Conquering
The Fear of Failure

By Madison Taylor

I0414144

Table of Contents

Introduction

You decide that you want to do something. You get excited about it, and you feel that you might have a shot at success. Just as you are about to make the plunge into your new dream or goal, a tiny little voice whispers, "What if you fail? People will laugh at you. You'll lose all the money you invested in this. You will look like a total fool." This voice grows louder and louder, until it is a panicked shout that drowns out the happier voice of encouragement that is also talking inside your head. Suddenly, you get discouraged, lost momentum, and even give up in the end. You let fear of failure stop you from achieving what you set your mind to. A mere little voice speaking a few worries that are not even grounded in reality scared you enough to make you give power to your fear and let go of power over your own life. How sad is that?

When you want to do something, the only thing stopping you is you. Your fear of failure can really hold you back from your dreams and your chances of success. While your fear of failure serves the very useful purpose of making you stick to wise choices, it can also hinder you from doing something really crazy and going after your dreams. This book will help you break down your fear of failure so that you can be successful instead.

Your fear of failure can seem like an impossible barrier. You may feel that you cannot possibly go against the intense tingling in your gut and the strong voices in your head that caution you no. But your fear of failure is entirely mental. By changing your mindset, you can truly overcome it. Without this fear in your way, you will feel free to accomplish whatever you want. This book will give you the tools necessary to counteract the disabling effects that the fear of failure can have on your psyche so that you can silence that silly voice of fear and achieve what you set your mind to. Imagine being able to just do what you want to do without being held back by your own scared mind?

This does not mean that your fear of failure will just go away. That fear may haunt you every step of the way on your journey through life. As human beings, we all have to face the fact that life carries many risks with it and that we all face the chance of failure; thus, life is scary at times and our natural fear can never be reasonably accepted to just completely disappear from our hearts one day. But you will at least be able to overcome the fear inside your heart and to act despite it. You can take charge of your own mental processes and emotions, and hence of your own success and the direction of your life. You can stop giving power to your fear, no matter how strongly you feel it.

Today, I want you to start reading this book and stop letting fear of failure prevent you from tackling what you have always wanted to achieve. Also stop thinking of your fear of failure as some useless part of yourself that you must fight, repress, and ignore. Your fear of failure is actually very useful to your life, but you must use it in a way that is constructive rather than limiting. By starting this book, you are taking the first step to actively disabling the limiting effects of your very natural fear of failure. By the end of this book, you will be in a position of true personal power. Then you can truly take on the world, even with your natural fear of failure whispering on and on inside of your mind.

Chapter 1: Understanding Your Fear

To overcome your fear of failure, you first must truly understand it. Your fear of failure is built into you. Understanding how it works and why it exists within your psyche can help you find out ways to work around it. It also helps you accept your fear as a normal and natural facet of your personality.

Symptoms of Fear of Failure

You may not even realize that you suffer from a fear of failure. All you know is that you get discouraged easily or have difficulties in bringing projects to completion. Maybe you procrastinate or quit a lot. You probably do have a fear of failure, lying under the surface of your commitment difficulties.

The first and foremost sign that you fear failure is if you want to do things, but the thoughts about what may go wrong and how you may fail make you stop. You may also think that you are not good enough to bring any project or dream to fruition. These beliefs make you develop tons of pipe dreams that you never ultimately complete. Instead of taking action, you just dream, then tell yourself that the dream is impossible and never really try to make it a reality.

Another sign is that the future may look dark to you. You are not sure if you will ever have the power or ability to create the future that you desire. You worry that you will fail everything so your future will not be good.

Do you look at your past and fixate on all of your failures? This indicates your deep internal belief that you are destined to fail since you have in the past. Your refusal to forgive yourself and move on shows that you do not believe in your ability to succeed anymore.

Your self-image may be very important to you. While your self-image is important, you should never exaggerate how you look to others. If you obsess over what others think of you to the point where you do not want to do things at the risk of looking stupid in front of others, then you fear the shame that accompanies failure.

This fear of shame is also indicated by your preoccupation with what others think of you. You worry that if you fail, you will lose relevance to other people. You fear that you will lose their interest, faith, and even love.

Finally, you worry that you will anger or disappoint people. The emotional reaction that you anticipate from others in the event that you fail is a major sign that you are terrified of letting others down.

You may also worry about shaming yourself. If you put a lot of pressure on yourself to be perfect, you can easily become disappointed. You are only human. Stop basing your worth and intelligence on how well you succeed at certain ventures.

You may also tell people "I don't expect to do very well at this" in order to lower their expectations and avoid disappointing them. You show people that you have no self-esteem or confidence in yourself when you do this and you also prove to yourself that you have no confidence. This sets you up for failure. But it is also a great indicator that you have a fear of failure based on a lack of confidence and belief in yourself.

Signs of nervousness right before you have to do something show that you have an intense fear of failure that manifests physically. You might get headaches or stomach issues the night before a big speech, for instance. Your nerves are from your ultimate fear of failure.

You may also use little tasks or life events as excuses to get distracted from your dream. You use these excuses so that you can lie to yourself and others that you are not actually giving up on your dream or pursuit by choice, that you really had to stop pursuing your dream for some legitimate reason. Usually, however, these reasons are not actually legitimate. They would not cause you to get distracted and give up if you really wanted to persevere.

Procrastination is a good sign that you have a fear of failure. You procrastinate in order to avoid reaching any sort of conclusion or completion that will prove whether you failed or succeeded. By procrastination, you are metaphorically hiding your head under a blanket to escape your fear of failure.

When you do fail, what is your attitude like? Do you think "Of course?" Do you just give up and stop trying to succeed? Do you find yourself unable to think of how you could have actually succeeded when you replay the failure? Do you maybe even feel relieved that you failed because it is what you expected to feel? If this is your attitude after a failure, then you definitely have a fear of failure working against you.

Why Fear is Normal

Here's a news flash: your fear of failure is totally normal. You are certainly not the only person in the world who quakes at the thought of failing. You also are not the only person who wants to avoid new experiences and risks because of this fear of possible failure. Fear of speaking is just one of many common manifestations of the fear of failure that haunts many people.

Neuro-linguistic programming and other psychology therapy methods like cognitive behavioral therapy promote the idea that nothing you do, think, or feel is actually useless. Your mind is pretty smart and it knows what it is doing. There is a valid reason for everything that it does. So when your fear of failure kicks in and starts to discourage you from your dreams, do not berate your mind for injecting a useless sense of fear into you. Your mind really believes that it is protecting you with a "voice of reason." Unfortunately, your mind does not understand that it is not really protecting you. Instead of hating your mind and yourself for experiencing a fear of failure, accept that this fear is natural and a part of a being human. Now view this fear as a useful tool that you can use to protect yourself as long as you apply it to your life in a more helpful way.

What exactly causes you to fly into shakes when you think that you might fail? Why is this fear so deeply profound and troubling? The power that the fear of failure has over people is certainly something that cannot be underestimated. After all, this fear of failure is responsible for so many people neglecting their dreams and giving up on their crazy ideas without so much as a single feeble attempt at success.

The answer is that your fear of failure is basically your human instinct. It is human instinct to not want to fail in life. This is because failure meant possible death for our ancestors. It also meant social alienation, which could result in death as well for our ancestors. When you fail, you can really hurt yourself financially, romantically, and otherwise. Failure also makes you look bad in front of others. Finally, it makes you look bad to yourself. Failure is a massive ego blow that can have hugely detrimental effects on your overall life.

Basically, fear of failure is not really a fear of failure. It is a fear of shame. Because of your instincts, you are basically hardwired to want others to respect you and love you. You need the support of your herd to feel safe and comfortable. You do not want to do anything that may earn you social rejection, because that meant certain death back in caveman times.

Even nowadays social alienation is very uncomfortable and unpleasant, even if it does not actually kill you. You want to do everything you can to avoid social rejection, so you try your hardest not to incur the shame or judgement of anyone else. You come to fear shame so much that it makes you avoid taking risks.

Fear of failure is also rooted in fear of unprecedented risk. When you take on some new risk or venture, you are facing a huge set of unknown consequences. You really cannot be one hundred percent certain that any of these consequences will be worth the return. However, it is better to find out rather than hanging out letting your life pass you by.

In caveman times, people had to work hard for food and shelter and basic survival.

Unorthodox moves in hunting, farming, and other survival attempts could endanger whole tribes. Therefore, anything unusual and unknown carried with it certain risk. That fact remains true today. If you try to do something unorthodox in your life, such as starting a new business based on a unique model, then you run a certain risk. This risk is naturally very frightening for you.

While most unorthodox moves and risks no longer carry the threat of imminent starvation or death at the maws of a terrifying prehistoric predatory creature, failure can still very much harm you. You probably have a lot to lose. When you think in those terms, it may appear that taking on any risk in your life is not worth taking. You stand to lose too much. You do not want to face life without the things that you care about, without money, without friends and family, without stability and security.

Fear of failure is thus even more deeply rooted in the natural human instinct to fear the unknown. You are doing something unprecedented with your life. You are taking on a risk that you never have before. The chances of your success are an unknown figure. Even if your chances are high, there is always some chance of failure if you make a mistake. But if you choose to look on the bright side, there is also always some chance of success no matter how high the risk of failure may be. Either way, it is normal to fear an unknown effect that something you do may have on your life. In fact, it is normal to be terrified!

At the heart, though, a fear of failure just means that you do not believe in yourself. You fear that you cannot do something and succeed. You fear that you are not adequate or skillful or smart or whatever enough to achieve what you have set your mind to. Your low self-esteem and lack of confidence makes you afraid of failure because you actually believe that failure is the most likely outcome of anything you try to do. One of the biggest themes of this book will be to encourage you to believe in yourself, while also changing your attitude about your fear of failure.

Why Others Seem Fearless

Do you know of anyone who seems totally fearless? Entrepreneurs who start crazy businesses on their last few dollars. Entertainers and public speakers who try new antics and tricks to get attention and entertain the masses. Outgoing party people who are not afraid to jump into a room and start talking to people. Slick bar prowlers who make it seem like nothing to walk up to someone at a bar or party and initiate sex or even a relationship. These people do things with unknown chances of success, and they do not ever bow down to their fear of failure. Even when failure seems more likely than success, they still make a move.

What is up with this? Are these people somehow born without the natural human fear of failure? Why are these people so fearless and how can you become more like them?

No one human being is totally immune to the fear of failure. It is bred into all people. Even the wildest, most daring entrepreneurs, socialites, and risk takers probably have a fear of failure somewhere inside of them when they set out on a new venture. But these people know better than to let their fear of failure stop them. They understand that the fear does not guarantee that they will fail, so they act anyway, and they may or may not succeed. When they do fail, they don't let their failures mess up their emotions or make them bitter, they simply move on and try again.

It isn't that these people are different from you in their fear of failure. They are probably just as scared of you. But they have developed a different attitude about failure that enables them to be gutsy and bold. You need to adopt elements of their healthy attitudes too. Use these people as role models for how you want to become when it comes to taking risks and chasing after dreams. Let them encourage and inspire you.

How to Make Your Fear Helpful Rather than Hindering

If you fear failure so much that it cripples you, then you are not in control. You need to gain control and then your fear of failure will not influence you so heavily. You can transform your innate and natural fear of failure into something helpful rather than hindering, but you just have to tweak your mindset about your fear a little bit.

While I will be covering ways to overcome your fear of failure and ensure your success in the following chapters, I wanted to first use this chapter to teach you how to improve your relationship with your fear of failure. It is helpful to view your mind as your best friend and the fear of failure that it brings up as a useful tool that your cautious friend likes to use to protect you from disaster. Don't hate yourself or your mind for being afraid; instead, be thankful and acknowledge the wisdom that your fear of failure may carry.

Even agree with this voice of reason that speaks inside your mind. Yes, there is actually a risk of failure in anything and everything that you do in life. Literally *everything*. You could fail just walking down the stairs; I'm sure you have stubbed your toes at least once in your lifetime. Minimalize the drama and horror of failure by acknowledging it and then trivializing it by remembering how common failure is and how it has never killed you.

Think about what you truly fear when it comes to failure. How bad are these things in real life? How legitimate are these worries? When you analyze your fear, you will find that some of your biggest worries are actually quite silly.

Also acknowledge the risks and the things that you need to be afraid of in your dream that are causing you so much fear. Make a plan to mitigate the risks so that you can feel safer and so that potential failure doesn't just destroy your quality of life should it actually happen.

All of this makes your fear seem less terrifying. Now your fear of failure seems like an old buddy now, right? It is something that is serving you a useful purpose in life.

Now, even after you have acknowledged all of the potential risks in your endeavors and made contingency plans, your internal fear may still linger. Fear is often a more physical feeling than mental, since fear triggers your brain to activate adrenalin for fight or flight. When your body is flooded with adrenalin, it doesn't just go away. You have to deal with that lingering fear sensation. Transform this fear sensation into the adrenalin rush sensation that you need to take on a big challenge. View life as a huge game, where you are constantly taking risks. The risks themselves are fun because of the adrenalin rushes that they give you. But the ultimate goal of the game is to not fail. You are playing for success. Keep your eye on success; challenge yourself to it. Let fear drive you, rather than inhibit you.

Once you do succeed, focus on that in the future more than the few times you fail. Know that you are capable of success. If you do happen to fail, view it as a challenge to do better next time and as a lesson on what not to do. Don't use failure as a reason to hate yourself and give up on your dreams. Live by the mantra, "If at first you don't succeed, try again."

Understand that your fear of failure is perfectly natural. It does not make you any less of a person. But it is only fear, something mental that goes on inside your mind. You can harness this fear and gain control over it if you simply adjust your attitude about it. The power really is within you. Use the seemingly "fearless" people in the world as assurance that it really is possible to gain control over your own fear.

Chapter 2: Actualize Success

Instead of just focusing on failure all of the time, it is a great idea to focus more on success. Think of the positive rather than the negative. As a result, you will start to feel that success is just as likely of a reality as failure is. Your fear will diminish and you will have more drive to just go for it! You can enjoy success, but only if you strive for it.

The human mind is infinitely powerful. If you choose to focus on failure, then your mind is more inclined to fail because that's what it is used to thinking about. Even thinking in negative terms like, "I better not fail at this," is still thinking about failure and putting the concept of failure into your mind. You want to avoid thinking about failure altogether by putting it out of your mind completely. Instead, make your mind think about success. Your mind will follow suit by subconsciously performing actions sure to bring you success.

How can you become more success-oriented? For one thing, you need to change your mentality. For another, you need to start acting in ways that invite success into your life. Make your life about success, not about fearing, hating, and avoiding failure.

Mentally Prepare for Success

I already talked a little bit about making your mind more positive by thinking about success as opposed to failure. Now I want to go more into depth about how to do this.

Visualize Success

It is a fantastic and helpful idea to visualize your success. Visualizing helps make things more real to your mind. It is better to visualize your desired outcome when you undertake some sort of venture. When you get paralyzed by your fear of failure, you probably unintentionally do the opposite. You spend more time envisioning how things could go wrong than how they could go right. But if you reverse that and actually focus more on what success will look like to you, then you are preparing your mind for success to be a reality. Your mind will thus accept this reality and work hard toward making it come true because that is what visualizing makes it believe that it is supposed to do.

So I want you to take a piece of paper. You can also go to the craft store and get a vision board that you can decorate. It doesn't matter how you do it, but you need to make your success visual and tangible for your brain to understand. First, what does success look like to you? Maybe it looks like owning a beach home, or like running a business with five employees and a hundred thousand a year income. Whatever it is, it is not silly, trust me. Just write it down, or draw it, or find a picture of it and put it on your vision board.

Second, I want you to spend at least five minutes a day envisioning your success in your mind, behind closed eyes. Daydream about it, though briefly. Too much daydreaming can cut into the time you need to proactively work toward your goals. Just daydream enough to make your desired outcome seem real to your mind.

Now, when you work on your project, don't envision all the ways it could fail. Just think solely about that successful end result that you have been envisioning. Visualize this end result as the outcome of your project, rather than any other result. When people ask you how your project is coming, just visualize how much closer you are to your desired outcome, and smile and tell them that your project is coming along great.

Think about Success

As I discussed above, it is very important for you to think in success terms, rather than failure terms. This subtle change in your thinking may not seem like a big deal, but it actually is. It will have a huge influence on what your mind tries to do and what your mind accepts as reality.

It is best to have only thoughts of success. Cut failure thoughts out of your thought process. Sometimes this will seem impossible, but you will just have to fake it. The more you fake it, the more easy thinking about success will become.

Start thinking about success more. When you work on your goal, think about how much closer you are getting to success. Think things like, "Today I got one step closer to my goal." Even if you seem very far away from your end goal, you are still making progress. That's better than doing nothing. If you do nothing, then your failure is truly guaranteed, but now you are just increasing your chances of success every day. You are essentially raising the odds.

Also, don't fixate on failure. When you start to think, "But what if I fail?" just redirect that thought into, "But what if I succeed?" Don't tell yourself not to fail; instead, tell yourself to succeed!

Instead of thinking about how to minimize or avoid failure, think about how to maximize and grow success. Focus on how to succeed and the steps you need to take for success. Sometimes it is useful and even necessary to consider taking steps to mitigate potential failures or problems, but your strategy for success should primarily be about growing success, not downsizing failure. Approach the strategy with a desire to win, rather than a desire to lessen the losses you will suffer when you lose.

Ultimately, I want you to just eliminate "failure" from your vocabulary. All you really need to think about is success and how to succeed. Challenge yourself to succeed, not to avoid failing. You will find this more positive and success-oriented thinking is great for changing your overall outlook on life and approach to achieving what you set your mind to.

Talk about Success

If you want to alter your thinking, you also need to alter how you speak. You need to start using more success terms in your speech, both to yourself and to other people. You will convince yourself and others that you are on the path to victory. People will feel and respect your confidence; your mind will believe that success is a definite possibility and will try harder to be successful.

Tell people how hard you are trying to succeed, not how hard you are trying not to fail. Tell people that you are taking certain steps to success, not that you are taking certain steps to avoid failure. People will believe in you more when they hear you talking about succeeding, not just avoiding failure. Try to leave the word "failure" out of every conversation you have with other people about what you are trying to achieve.

Also talk like you are sure to succeed. Even if your gut is quaking and you are more certain that you will fail, do not admit this to others. You do not want to give away your lack of confidence, or people will lose confidence in you too and you will have less support getting to your success. Talk like you are sure of yourself. You will start to believe it, as will everyone else. And heartfelt, genuine confidence is always the key to success.

When you speak, choose to use forward, positive terms. By this I mean say things like, "I *will* do this" and "I am *working on* this." When someone asks you how your project is going, tell them how it is moving forward and how you have met certain milestones. It is all about forward progress when it comes to success. Convince yourself that your project is headed for success by viewing it as a forward-moving work in progress.

Appreciate the Bright Side

Say you have just opened up a new restaurant and you are really scared that it is going to fail because the restaurant industry is cutthroat. Today one of your fryers broke which you don't have the money to fix yet and a customer criticized your steak, even threatening that he will leave a bad review. Also today someone wrote a very wonderful blurb about your establishment in a local foodie journal, which should drive some traffic your way, and you finally hired on the perfect waitress. Two bad things that could lead to your failure happened; also two good things that could lead to your success happened. Both have pretty equal weight. So which do you choose to focus on?

Humans are naturally programmed to focus on the negative. After all, the negative can have the deepest impact on your life, so it is a good idea to always notice and try to fix problems. However, sometimes humans fixate a little too much on negative things that are really not so bad. They choose to notice the negative over the positive.

If you have a fear of failure, refer to the example above. Maybe you are choosing to fixate on the bad things, the potential causes of failure, over the good things, the potential causes of success? Maybe your chances of success are just as high or possibly even higher than your chances of failure, but you don't see that because you are so focused on the negative all of the time. By missing out on seeing your chances and windows for success because of your fixation on the negative, you instead devote all of your energy to how you might fail. You essentially neglect your success as a result.

By focusing instead on the positive signs of potential success, you actually increase your chances of success. You devote more energy to growing your chances of success than your chances of failure. In addition, you feel better because you see that you are not just blindly failing. You realize that you actually stand a chance and that your efforts are not all in vain.

Let's go back to our example. As the aspiring restauranteur, you could feel like your business is failing. Or you could appreciate the good things that happened during the day and welcome in new customers from the foodie journal and appreciate your new waitress. Then, instead of just assuming that your problems will make you fail, use your success to fix your problems. Use the new customers' money to help fix the fryer and the new waitress to help appease the angry customer. By this example, you can see how you can really grow your success by focusing on it rather than focusing on the bad things.

Take Control

When you fear failure, you lose a little bit of control over your emotions and ultimately of your life. You want to keep control. When you start to feel control sliding away, just choose not to think too much about what is out of your control. You will never be able to control or micro manage everything, so do not even bother trying. Instead, make yourself feel better by focusing on what you do have control over. Focusing on these things will help you feel grounded and more in control, and as a result you will naturally act in a more controlling and confident way.

You have control over yourself, right? Even if it doesn't feel like it at times, you really do. You can control your thoughts, your speech, and even your actions. Use this self-control to help control how you approach success. Use it to cultivate success.

Also look at aspects of your goals that you have control over. Maybe you can't control other people or money or the stock market or the weather, but you can control what work is done each day or what supplies you get. You can control who you involve in your project with you.

45

There will be plenty of times when you feel totally powerless. Your control over your life truly seems dead. Again, it is perfectly OK to fake it until you believe it. Convince yourself and others that you do have control. Take control of what you can, put a smile on, and exert the aura that you are someone who is in control of your own life. Things will start to fall into place the more you keep up this act and try to gain control over what you can.

Don't fight things that refuse to bend to your control, however. There are many things in life that you can't control. Instead of wasting your time on these things, try to take control of what you can control. Give up and stop fighting the things that are outside of your jurisdiction in life.

Take back your control and use it. You will feel better in the end.

Cultivate Successful Habits

Do you ever read those articles in periodicals like Forbes that describe what the most successful people in the world do? If not, you should. These articles may seem silly, but in reality, they are handing you keys to success. The idea is, the people that the articles are about are already successful. They must be doing something right. Emulating their behavior and habits is thus sure to help you become more successful too. I agree and I am going to share some activities and habits that successful people swear by. Adopt these habits, and you will become more successful in all areas of life.

Take Your Time

Flying around in a constant rush does not do anyone any good. Taking your time and methodically handling each and every one of your goals is really the best way to live. Successful people know that they need to take their time to do the job right the first time around. Learn from them and stop rushing things. Take as much time as you need to do something right the first time. Your quality of work will soar, as will your success. Patience is indeed a virtue. Keep that in mind; write it down if you must.

Write Down Tips

So let me guess. You have found some great wisdom in these pages, and in the pages of other book and articles as well. You highlight the most useful passages for later reference. But in time, you forget these tips and you never revisit the highlighted passages. It is better to commit these tips to memory by writing them down or copying and pasting them to an Evernote page. Then, revisit the page now and then to remind yourself how to better lead your life.

I also find that fortune cookie wisdom can actually have a great effect on your overall success. Tape particularly profound fortune cookie messages to your laptop, desk, or wall. Maybe even create a collage filled with wise quotes and motivational messages that will inspire you to be successful at life.

Spend Time with Family

Truly successful people understand that play is just as important as work. They understand that you need to be emotionally and spiritually fulfilled, neither of which can be achieved by working only. Thus, successful people know that it is important to dedicate time to loved ones and emotionally fulfilling activities with loved ones.

If you want to be successful, embrace the non-work-related parts of life, particularly your friends and family. Give these people the time and love that they deserve. Enjoy what time you do have with them. Life moves fast and you want to enjoy time with your loved ones before they are gone.

Manage Your Time

Time management may be the most important thing that you can do to be successful. You cannot reasonably expect yourself to succeed if you have no idea what you are doing with your time. Successful people have schedules written in planners and online calendars that help them stay on track.

Start good time management. Never forget an appointment or task again by writing everything down. And I mean *everything*. Keep a daily planner and fill out the next day at the end of each day. Also consult the planner in the morning in order to frame your day in your mind, and in order to remind yourself of any appointments or deadlines. Also review your planner throughout the day.

Set alarms on your phone at least an hour before appointments. Always leave early so that you have time to contend with unexpected delays, such as traffic jams or forgetting your wallet. You know how these things always happen when you are in a hurry, so remove the hurry from your routine.

Have a Routine

A routine helps you organize your day so that you get everything done. It also helps you manage your time because your body knows just what to do and when. Your body will become healthier with a routine and your mind will become quieter. You will have less stress and anxiety.

One of the most common habits of successful people is to get up early. Quit hitting the snooze button and roll out of bed at least at six a.m., at the latest. Start your day proactively with yoga or some other energizing workout, a protein-rich breakfast, and positive thinking. This will suck at first, but as time wears on, you will be amazed at how much you can accomplish by rising early. It will suddenly feel like you have several extra hours in your day.

Your routine should also include meal times, eight hours of sleep, and some exercise. These things keep you healthy. Successful people know that they cannot be successful and run on their top efficiency without their health intact. If you look at the diets of truly successful people, they usually eat quite well. Consider salads on the go when you are busy working, so you can stay healthy without spending tons of dough and taking lots of time out of your day to eat well.

Plan Ahead

Successful people are grounded in the present, yes. But they do dedicate some time to thinking of certain possible scenarios. As a result, they are prepared for the future. They are not caught by surprise.

Adopt this trait. Try to plan a few spaces ahead in the chess game of life. Consider all sorts of scenarios, both good and bad. Have fallback plans for potential failure. Don't fixate on the possibility of failure, however. Just try to be proactive about preventing failure. Try to remain unemotional about the scenarios you envision.

Quiet Your Mind

Successful people know that the anxiety and other junk that flies around in their brains all of the time is exhausting, distracting, and worthless. So they know to quiet their minds throughout the day. It is not unusual to find corporate executives and CEOs taking time to volunteer, meditate, do yoga, run in the park, or otherwise enjoy themselves and give their minds time to unwind.

Do things that quiet your own mind by giving you a joyful purpose in life without just thinking about all of your worries and cares. Volunteering is always a great option because then you can feel like you are making a positive difference in the world. A hobby is also great as it infuses joy into your life. Physical exercise gives you energy, stamina, focus, and mental clarity. Whatever you decide to do, don't feel guilty about taking a few minutes to a few hours out of your day to do something besides work. You will actually find that it improves your concentration and makes you more successful.

Try NLP Training

There is a good reason that neuro-linguistic programming is so wildly popular among corporate training teams and management training organizations. Many people trump the success of NLP as a means for unlocking your inner potential and improving your ability to communicate and work well with others.

If you can find an NLP coach or training seminar, by all means take advantage of it. NLP can really help you learn how to be successful using the tools and attitudes that you already possess internally. NLP believes that you already have what it takes to be successful, but things like your fear of failure has locked that potential away. Break out of your mental traps and unlock your unlimited potential through NLP hypnosis and visualization techniques.

Limit Emails and Social Media

Instead of being constantly accessible to people, you should limit your contact with others. This frees you from social distraction and lets you concentrate on the task at hand more thoroughly. Only check email and social media a few times a day. Have a set time in your routine for these things.

That does not mean that you need to be anti-social. Successful people know the power and importance of healthy social interaction. You just have to limit your social interaction to when you have time. There is a time and a place for everything. Socializing should not mix with work or projects.

Practice Makes Perfect

One way to mitigate your chances of failure is to actually become great at what you want to do. If you are trying to start a new business or master a new skill, practice it to death. Metaphorically, of course. Practice and dedicate all of your time to this new skill. Learn

58

all that you can. Immerse yourself in the new world that you wish to be a part of. This dedication will make you so good at your new skills or industry that you will be more successful, guaranteed.

Successful people also never stop practicing and never stop learning. You can always teach an old dog new tricks, never mind how the saying goes. The only way to advance yourself in life and continue to be successful is to ensure your relevance in life. Keep learning new things. Even if you already know something, keep studying and practicing it. Take it from athletes and martial artists: you can never get too good at something. Staying relevant by practicing and learning new relevant skills are a great way to continue and even increase your chances of success at any venture.

Be Accountable

One big difference between successful people and non-successful people is that successful people are personally accountable. They believe that their success is entirely their own responsibility. They do not rely on others to make them successful. They also do not blame others for their mistakes and failures.

Your success is entirely your doing. Only you can accomplish true success. Stop giving power to others by relying on them, waiting for them, and blaming them. You will be sorely disappointed if you rely on others, because other people are not here exclusively to help and serve you. You need to go after what you want and take the actions necessary for success. Only you can ensure that you do what you need the way you need it done. So rely exclusively on yourself.

However, this does not mean that you cannot be a team player. Successful people also understand how important it is to work with others and to use others to reach a common goal. Having a good team and using the help of others is not a bad idea to reach your own success at all. Just don't rely on others to do everything for you and to carry you to success. That is your job only.

Be Decisive

This ties into the previous tip. Your decisions are what lay the foundation for your action and your success. That means that you need to be very decisive. Wavering and deliberating slowly over decisions wastes time and causes you to overthink, which can lead to you making mistakes. Instead, be quick and firm in the decisions that you make. Make your own decisions, without relying on others to make decisions for you. Everyone has different ways of doing things; if you rely on others to make decisions for you, you will ultimately make a decision that behooves the people you asked, not yourself. It is OK to consult others for advice, but ultimately you need to make decisions yourself.

Once you make a decision, you may be riddled with doubt. But so what? Remember that you made your decision for a good reason and stick by it. Commit to your decisions. If you made a bad decision, you can change it later.

However, changing your mind a lot will lead you to making mistakes and losing the respect of others. You need to stick decisions out until it is obvious that they are not working out. Only make a change when you see that it is clearly necessary.

Be Open-Minded

Having a closed mind is not the hallmark of a successful person. Being open to new ideas and ways of doing things is far more conducive to your success. Even at the risk of failure, be daring enough to try new things and challenge the status quo. You might just find that something unusual or unprecedented is the perfect solution to reaching your goal.

In addition, you need to be open-minded about other people. Let go of personal biases and judgements, as these can make you reject people and ideas that are actually very helpful. You do not have to let go of your personal beliefs, but you do have to set those beliefs aside when working with others. Customers, co-workers, and supervisors are all examples of people that you may have to work with. You cannot create an easy and successful work environment if you are always butting heads with other people because of their various differences from you. By being close-minded, you will just alienate people and make your success harder to reach.

Embrace Challenges

Successful people view setbacks and failures as challenges, not sources of doom. They enjoy figuring out how to conquer challenges and still succeed. They even make a game of it.

Stop being negative and sensitive. Turn humps in your goals into fun challenges that you must solve. Make your goals an ending point that you must reach no matter what, and then never give up on reaching your goals. View challenges as steps in the whole process, not as insurmountable hindrances and stop signs.

X Marks the Spot

To help show yourself your high level of forward progress, get a wall calendar. Now, mark a huge red X through every day that you have worked on your goal. Leave days that you haven't worked on your goal blank. Seeing blank days will start to bother you, and you will feel motivated to fill every day with a big red X. This is a great way to motivate yourself and get a lot of work done. In the end, when you complete your goal, you can look at how many days you worked on it and you will feel a great sense of pride.

Chapter 3: Overcome Your Fear of Failure

By now, you know that I advocate not dismissing or repressing your fear of failure. Your fear of failure is a useful part of your psychological makeup that you must embrace fully. But how can you do this? Also, how can you move forward in life while your fear continues to haunt you behind your smile? Basically, when you are so scared of failure that you want to quit, it can be hard to continuc with your dreams. But it is necessary that you not let your fear take away your drive and your happiness. Take power by using the following tips to help lessen and even overcome your fear of failure.

A.W.A.R.E.

A.W.A.R.E. is an acronym that helps you remember the steps crucial for overcoming your fear of failure. Each letter of the acronym stands for an important step. The overall acronym also reminds you to maintain awareness of your emotions, which helps you overcome the fear. Ignoring your fear is not helpful; acknowledging and accepting the fear and working with it is far more helpful.

A = Accept Anxiety

In other words, own your fear. Stop rejecting it, denying it, or repressing it. Accept and acknowledge that it exists – and for a good reason. You are afraid, OK? You have every reason to be afraid. That fear is normal and it is acceptable. It does not make you any less of a person. However, it also doesn't make you its slave. You can still act, whether that fear exists within you or not.

W = Watch the Anxiety

Watch the anxiety.

A = Act Normally

Sometimes, you just have to fake it. Even if you want to puke because you are so nervous, just put a smile on and act normally. That will ultimately still your troubled nerves and help you move forward because it will convince your brain that everything is normal and there is no need for the nervousness. Acting normally will also make other people respect you more and they will give you more positive support if you appear to be normal.

If you need to express your fear, do it to a close loved one, counselor, or journal. Do not tell the people that you are in business with or people that you are not extremely close to.

R = Repeat Above Steps

These steps can be repeated until your fear is truly gone. There is no shame in going through these steps in your mind over and over until you feel calm.

E = Expect the Best

Go ahead and expect the best. Be optimistic. Invite success by openly expecting it. Show others your confidence by being optimistic, as well. If you notice, politicians are always optimistic. This helps their voters feel more confident as well. You will make yourself and everyone else believe in your success if you are optimistic and if you believe in yourself.

Mental Exercises

There are mental exercises that you can perform to help minimize your sensation of fear so that you can function. These are especially useful when you are flying into a panic attack or before you must do something where you might fail, such as a speech, performance, or business idea proposal.

Visualization

Close your eyes tight. Think about the situation that terrifies you. Imagine yourself hitting some sort of obstacle which can lead to your ultimate failure. Now let yourself feel your fear consume you. But even though you are afraid, you know that this is just a visualization, so you can move forward. Move forward mentally. Figure out how to overcome obstacles in the future without feeling the terror and panic filling your body. This visualization trains your brain to abandon fear in favor of problem solving.

Breathing

Right before an event or activity where you might fail, you might suffer from terrible nerves. Breathing deep into your diaphragm, slowly releasing the air through your nose, and then breathing in again three times can really help dispel your terrible sense of nerves. Really focus on your breath to take your mind off of your fear.

Tapping

Tapping also works to distract you from your nerves and ground you in the present moment so that you have the best mental clarity for a task. When you use tapping, take your middle and forefingers and start tapping an area on your body. Between the forefinger and thumb, under the ear, and on the collarbone are great places that work for a lot of people because they are tender areas. Tap three times while saying an affirmation, such as "I will do well at this."

Progressive Muscle Relaxation

Ground yourself in the present and relax yourself by going through your entire body. Start in your right-hand thumb. Tense the muscle in your thumb, then force it to relax. Now travel up your right arm, down the right side of your body, and then up the left side of your body. Be sure to relax the muscles on your face and scalp as well. Conclude with your left-hand thumb. You may repeat this as necessary until you feel calm and present-minded. Also, be sure to breathe in and out and focus on your breathing as you perform progressive muscle relaxation.

Positive Affirmations

Positive affirmations can psyche you up. I cover them again in the chapter about believing in yourself, so head to Chapter 4 for instructions. Use these affirmation when your fear of failure peaks or before a big event that you are scared about.

Make Failure into a Learning Experience

Failure does suck. I won't even try to sugar coat it. The various fallouts from a failure can range from minor to major, but they are never pleasant. Perhaps the worst blow from failure is to your own ego. You tend to feel that you let others down, even if you did not, and you feel that you are inadequate and unable to make your own dreams into reality.

But failure does offer you something more valuable than just pain: It offers learning experiences. Inside every failure is a huge message about what does not work. If you pay attention to these lessons, you can gain a better understanding of what you need to do differently in the future in order to enjoy more success.

It can hurt to analyze your failure, but try to remove the ego and the emotional connection to your failure and observe it objectively. You can even go over it with someone else. Try to glean what you can from this failure.

Many people think that failure or success are two opposite possibilities for every venture or attempt that you make in life. But usually they actually run parallel. Failure gives birth to success; and sometimes, even when you enjoy some type of success, you failed at some part of your venture and managed to bounce back or redirect your efforts into something more fruitful. The two are intertwined and cannot exist without one another. So embrace failure as a valid part of success and use it to actually ensure your success.

Stop Comparing Your Present to Your Past

Living in the past is one of the hugest reasons why you may have a fear of failure. Past events have scarred you and lowered your self-esteem. You may think that you fail at everything because you have been through a divorce or you are repeatedly rejected by romantic partners, you repeatedly aren't hired by the job that you want, and a past business venture failed. While it is understandable that your brain is now afraid for you to suffer any more in the face of rejection and failure, do not let your brain form false associations between your past and your present. Just because you experienced failure is the past does not at all translate into any factual truth that you will fail again in the future.

Really look at your failures. Learn from them, but also realize how they differ from what you are trying to do now. For example, a past divorce has nothing to do with your new girlfriend or boyfriend, because this new partner is a whole different person. For another example, a divorce has nothing at all to do with starting a bakery.

In addition, notice the differences between your past and your present. Realize how you have changed and grown as a person. Acknowledge new skills and life lessons that you have acquired in order to achieve better success. Actually recognize how your situation is different. And ditch these silly beliefs that you are somehow not good enough or that you are doomed to fail for the rest of your life.

Embrace the Fear

It is sometimes better to view ventures as fun risks rather than scary unknowns. Make the unknown aspect of new undertakings something exhilarating rather than scary. Sure, you have no idea what your chances are for success. But if you did know, would that really make it better? If you knew that your business idea had a huge chance of failure, you probably would never risk it. As a result, you would miss out on the tiny chance of success. In addition, you would miss out on the important life lessons and other parts of the experience of launching your business that will inevitably occur, whether or not you enjoy success in the end. Half of the fun of life is not knowing what is going to happen, but doing it anyway. Life is about the journey more than the end result. So enjoy the journey and quit worrying about how successful you are going to be.

Start to change your attitude about success and failure. This truly will lessen the fear, or at least the vise grip that the fear may have on your action. View challenges and risks as things to surmount, not as stop signs or reasons to give up. Try to inject some fun into figuring out how to navigate failures and increase your success in the end.

It is a bad idea to think in black or white terms. Instead, think in gray terms. Something may be bad and may spell your failure – but it may be good too. Try to locate the good in everything and use the good to your advantage. Do everything you can to flip problems and failures into successes. Usually there is a way to find the good in something bad and make it better. Dedicate your time to finding solutions to obstructions and problems, rather than hanging your head in shame and giving up.

Nothing in life is ever easy, especially good things. Seeing the results of hard work and perseverance is the most rewarding experience that you will ever enjoy in your entire life. You will gain the hugest and most satisfying sense of pride when you overcome opposition and turn a failure into a success. Therefore, you need to try to make your dreams come true and you need to try to work through every failure. You should never let fear of failure hold you back. Instead, enjoy the ride and the hard work that it takes to reach your ultimate goal.

Ignore the Fear

Yes, this advice is the polar opposite of what I just said. But sometimes, if your fear is truly groundless and silly, then there is no point embracing it. It does not serve you at all. So just ignore it. Instead of focusing on this fear, just redirect your thoughts in another direction. When the fear bubbles up in your brain, start thinking about success, or about Grand Ma's apple pie, or about whatever gets your mind totally off of your fear.

Challenge Yourself in a Different Area of Life

Challenge yourself in a different area of life to prove to yourself that you can be successful. Enroll in a Tough Mudder competition or a boot camp challenge at a local fitness center. Try Team Beach Body home workouts. Enroll in some sort of class, even just a creative beading or pottery class. Take puzzles or go to adult spelling bees. Whatever it is that you decide to do, make sure that it challenges you. Also make sure that it has absolutely nothing to do with your venture or current undertaking that has you filled with fear of failure. When you see yourself succeed, you will feel the true glory of your abilities, and you will be thrilled. You will now have the skills of persistence and the taste of success to drive you to completing your venture.

Counseling

Sometimes, counseling can be necessary, particularly when you suffer from insurmountable, debilitating fear of failure known as "Kakorrhaphiophobia." You don't have to know how to pronounce to know whether or not you have it. If you simply cannot act in life because of your crippling fear of failure, then you have a phobia. This phobia calls for treatment because it is seriously lowering your quality of life. A counselor can help expose you to challenges so that you overcome the phobia, step by step.

Even if you are not suffering a severe phobia, sometimes counseling can help you get over hang-ups and negative thought patterns that prevent you from achieving what you set your mind to. A counselor can help get to the root of why you are so afraid of failure. He or she can help you see how your beliefs and your fears are actually hindering you and how you can work through them by redirecting your thoughts.

Chapter 4: Believe in Yourself

Have you ever heard of atelophobia? Most people have not, yet this phobia affects countless people. It is a form of anxiety where you are haunted by the sense that you are not good enough and you fear imperfection. It is classified as an anxiety disorder and many psychologists refer to it as a form of neurotic perfectionism. For most people with a fear of failure, some degree of atelophobia is responsible. You fear that you are not good enough to succeed; failure seems like such a likelihood to you that you think you stand no chance. You worry that you will somehow "mess it up, like always."

You need to believe in yourself. While I know this is hard, it is certainly possible. I will tell you how.

Accept You're Not Everyone's Cup of Tea

Not everyone in the world is going to like you. Don't let this fact get to you or make you doubt yourself at all. Just because someone doesn't like you does not mean that you are somehow unworthy or a bad person. The opinions of others who do not really know you have no real bearing on your life. It is also quite possible to work with people without any sort of affectionate bond or connection. You can be professional and cordial. You don't have to be best friends to still have value to the other person and to get things done. So don't measure your worth by others' standards and do not let others inject you with doubt.

Identify and Rationalize Doubts

What are your main doubts? Why do you have them? Figure out what they are and why they are not true. Reason through your doubts and disprove all the bad things that you believe about yourself.

Stop Listening to Negative People

Surround yourself with people who talk you up. Do not waste time with negative people who only seem to discourage you. A lot of your self-doubts likely come from others, so be careful who you let influence you.

Improve Your Self-Talk

The way you talk to yourself has a huge effect on your self-esteem. You probably say horrific things to yourself that you would never say to people that you care about. Well, you need to stop doing this to yourself. Speak to yourself like you would a friend in order to grow your self-esteem and confidence. You have to live with yourself for the rest of your life, so you might as well be pleasant to be around. Stop being your own worst enemy and growing your own doubts.

Pretend to Be Confident

Sometimes you got to talk the talk to walk the walk. Pretending to be confident can make you appear so to others. As they come to respect you more, you may come to respect yourself more. Then your confidence becomes actually real.

It is a good idea to speak positively about yourself. Do not tear yourself down or portray yourself to others in a negative light. Do not make self-deprecating jokes, no matter how funny they may be. Do not constantly say sorry for everything and let people interrupt you. Also, speak clearly, without saying "Um" a lot. Use a good vocabulary. Hold yourself in a confident posture, too, with your head held high, your spine straight, your shoulders back, and your arms relaxed at your sides with your hands open, not clenched in fists. Resist urges to fidget, bite your nails, or otherwise nervously groom yourself. You will appear confident and your actions will make you feel confident, too.

It is also best to speak first. Introduce yourself to people first rather than waiting for an introduction. This makes you appear like a go-getter.

Recall Your Successes

One of the best ways to erase self-doubt and increase self-faith is to recall your past successes. It may be easier to dwell on ways that you have failed in the past, but this just tears you down. Instead, think about what you have done well and successfully. Maybe you made captain of a school sports team, graduated with honors, rescued an abused pet, made a delicious dinner, or bought a home all with your own money? Maybe you get a broken-down car to start running again or you get an A on an incredibly hard exam that you were certain that you had flunked? No matter how small it may seem, all of your successes matter. Use them as proof to yourself that you can succeed if you put your mind to it.

Chapter 5: The Greatest Failures in the World

Failure is not the end of the world. Some of the greatest inventors and entrepreneurs in our history were at first failures. For inspiration, read about some of these massive historical failures that eventually turned into brilliant successes. If these people could bounce back after a failure, then so can you. Use these people as inspiration to persevere with your dreams and lessen your fear of failure. After all, failure is not the worst thing that could happen to you and it does not mean that your dreams need to die.

J.K. Rowling

The multimillionaire literary genius that wrote the Harry Potter series is now a household name. She was a broke single mother who hand wrote most of the original Harry Potter drafts, and she experienced countless rejections from publishers. Just when she was about to throw her manuscript in the trash, she was accepted. Now look where she is. In a speech, she described failure as the one thing that stripped away all of her fear. She saw that even after the worst things imaginable happened to her and she had failed at every part of life, she was still alive. So why not keep trying to make it as an author? Use her story as inspiration to use failure as motivation for persistence and perseverance.

Steve Jobs

Jobs boldly started Apple in his garage. But at first, this household technology name floundered and almost drowned. Their computer sales were so poor that Jobs was actually fired by Apple. Apple continued to struggle and almost went under as Microsoft soared to success. Jobs observed how Microsoft was winning the tech industry over by being more innovative and keeping current with society's technology needs, and so when he got a second chance at Apple in 1997, he used the lessons from his failure to lead Apple into flourishing success as a tech great. Use him as inspiration to learn from your failure and still press on.

Walt Disney

Can you believe that Walt Disney was once fired from a newspaper for "lack of creativity"? Then he started Laugh-O-Gram, an animation company that rapidly went under. He tried his luck in Hollywood and kept receiving rejection after rejection. Then, suddenly, he managed to create some animated films that became the household names they are today. Use Walt Disney as inspiration to keep trying, even when you face rejection, because while some people just don't appreciate what you have to offer, that does not mean that you are not worth anything. You may just be an undiscovered gem, so keep plowing on.

Milton Hershey

The iconic Hershey bar was invented by Milton Hershey. But he wasn't always a staple on every store's candy shelf. He was first fired as a printer and then he launched three different candy companies, all of which failed. Yet somehow he got it right with Hershey Milk Chocolate Bars. He knew that milk chocolate would gain popularity so he pushed for it and finally his vision turned into a massive success. Use him as inspiration to believe in yourself. You may just have the right idea, even if you fail at first.

Abraham Lincoln

Abraham Lincoln is known as one of our founding fathers in America, and also as a visionary president elected in 1860. But before his major political contributions to the birth of the United States of America, Lincoln would appear like a bit of a loser. He lost many businesses, suffered a nervous breakdown, became a widower, and lost several elections into Congress. For some reason, he persevered, and is now an American legend. Use Lincoln as inspiration to keep trying, no matter what, because the longer you try, the more your odds

of succeeding rise.

Conclusion

Now you have reached the end of this book. In these pages, you have hopefully learned to believe in yourself, to focus on your success, to adopt successful habits, and to ditch your fear of failure. With these life skills, you can now tackle anything that you set your mind to. You do not need to cower in fear and let your life pass you by because you are too scared to try anything new.

Some of the biggest successes in history were once failures. Keep that in mind when your fear of failure begin to engulf you. You may fail, yes. Or you may succeed. You never will know if you do not at least try. If you do fail, at least you can get back up and try again, with fresh lessons in your mind. You will raise your odds of success the more you persevere.

Your fear of failure is your brain's attempt to keep you safe. It serves a great purpose so harness it and listen to it. But never make the mistake of letting this fear wrap you in a cocoon of safety that prevents you from ever achieving your dreams and really living your life. You will wake up old one day and realize that you never made any of your dreams come true, simply because you were scared of things that do not truly matter in the end.

It is important to focus on success over failure. Be more positive and become more success-oriented. Ultimately, this will manifest in your behavior. It is also important to adopt successful habits so that your lifestyle invites success in like a welcome guest. You need to make some adjustments to your life and your attitude if you want to see changes in your level of success.

It is also important to analyze your fear. What is truly worth being scared of? Will it even matter in a year or in thirty years? If not, go for it. Stop giving fear power, and instead take the power into your own hands. Learn from some of the greats on how to turn your fear of failure into adrenalin and exhilaration to defeat adversary in your life.

Sometimes you just need to take a deep breath. Let it all out. Appreciate life around you. And go for what you want. You can accomplish anything that you set your mind to, if you just really try.

Thank you so much for reading. This book truly will help you succeed at life and overcome your fear of failure, so read it as many times as you need to. Understand that the real power is within you, however, and use that power.

Other great books by Madison Taylor on Kindle, paperback and audio

Rejection Proof Therapy 101: How To Overcome, Deal With And Heal Yourself From Rejection

Cognitive Behavioral Therapy For Beginners: How To Use CBT To Overcome Anxieties, Phobias, Addictions, Depression, Negative Thoughts, And Other Problematic Disorders

Forbidden Psychology 101: The Cool Stuff They Didn't Teach You About In School

Escaping the Introvert World: The Introvert's Guide To Overcoming Shyness, Social Anxiety, And Fear To Thrive In An Extrovert World

NLP For Beginners: Learn the Secrets of Self Mastery, Developing Magnetic Influence and

Reaching Your Goals Using Neuro-Linguistic
Programming

Depression Proof Yourself: How To Avoid And
Overcome Being Depressed

Love Thyself: The First Commandment to
Raising your Self Esteem, Boosting your Self-
Confidence, and Increasing your Happiness

The Art of Decision Making: How to Make Better
Choices in Love, Life, and Work

The Dark Science of Psychological Warfare: How
To Always Keep The Upper Hand On Anyone
Psychologically

Staying Focused: How to Effectively Eliminate
the Weapons of Mass Distraction

Turbo Charged NLP: A New and Improved Way
of Taking Self Mastery, Influence, and Neuro-
linguistic Programming to the Next Level

The Art of Deception: How To Master And Use
Subterfuge On Anyone

How to Deal with Difficult People

www.ingramcontent.com/pod-product-compliance
Lightning Source LLC
Chambersburg PA
CBHW050411290526
45786CB00003B/1218